The Widov

and other poems

To Zoë and Mark and family

Barbara Howerska

The Widow Witch

and other poems

HALF
MOON
BOOKS

Published by Half Moon Books 2019
An imprint of OWF Press Community Interest Company
Otley Courthouse, Courthouse Street
Otley, West Yorkshire LS21 3AN

www.owfpress.com
www.halfmoonbooks.co.uk

Cover photo: © Liz O'Connell
Cover layout by Nick Palmer.

ISBN 978-1-9993036-4-8

Printed and bound by ImprintDigital.com, UK

Contents

Acknowledgements

'Biro on cardboard' was published in *Shadow Chest* (Beehive Poets, 2018).

'Voices' was written for *Bradford Refugee Week* and was performed by Bradford schoolchildren in June 2016 at Margaret McMillan Tower.

'The many love letters of Rosa Luxembourg' was written for the forthcoming drama, *AMOS*, Autumn 2019.

Many thanks to Mark Guest, Elizabeth O' Connell, Mike Farren, Char March, Peter White and all at Half Moon Books.

In Slavic mythology, the natural world is inhabited by magical spirits. Asrai are water spirits. Auka is a forest spirit and a Volkolak is the name given to a shape-changing spirit, who changes into a wolf.

The Widow Witch

The spell

Five maidens and fair widows three danced in the moonlight
around a tree,
ran through the village by candlelight, chosen to bless , for a
harvest ripe,
ran through the village all naked be, no one should look, no
one should see.

There's always one, a boy so free, he did so, did so want to see.

He opened the shutters, the shutters tight, to glimpse the
beauty in the night.
The moonlight broke, a thousand splinters cracked, foretold of
icy winters.
Rudi left the village late at night, into the snow and the white
moonlight.

Earth gave no flowers, no fruit or yield, the rabbits frozen in
the field.

Walked to the forest near mountains high, watching the eagle
circle the sky.
The wolf-eye glinted in the snow, moonlight dripping down
below.
Wolf with a tail with a patch of white, white in the tail in the
black moonlight.

Asrai

Skin biting cold, he trudged the crunching snow,
deep in the ancient forest, oak trees stood.
They sheltered him, their mighty columns high
from snow and ice, through earthen bowl of wood.

Rudi was young, but knew the wolf by name
a Volkolak, a creature turned by shape,
swifter than wolf and greater in all sense,
fear in the belly, eating his escape.

Spirit of wolf, the changing Volkolak
could be a wooded plant, a passing mouse,
then to a sleek and oily, snarling beast,
hiding in shadowed corners of a house.

Glad of the Emperor – the great north tree,
Rudi sat down, the hungry wolf nearby.
Asrai, the silver water-ones, looked on
and whispered, from the river to the sky.

The river spirits told of their delight.
Asrai could save him – keep him safe from harm,
his heart, his hand, his fingertips to touch
their silver robes, wrapped in the river's charm.

Now like a fish that darts in water clear,
cool in the soft and silken spirit calm,
Rudi dipped in the beams of glowing light,
a golden foil around him wrapped its charm.

Swirling and deeper, deeper down he went,
flying through water, breathing water – strange.
Opening eyelids slowly, this dark world
of patterns rushing by, of so much change.

Rudi saw walls with curling snakes and vines,
animals, plants and eyes on painted wood.
Honeyed, the pillars brown went rushing by,
reaching a great hallway in which he stood.

Dry, dusty air, yet clothes were stuck to skin.
Fire in the hearth was burning, red with flame.
Tall woman stood, with skin that looked like bronze,
green dress of leaves and hair of horses' mane.

Bending an arm, she turned towards a door,
her fingers long, her body in an arc.
Somehow he stumbled forward to her shape
Asrai, she whispered, *but beware the auk.*

Auka, the forest joker, likes to play.
This Rudi thought, as feeling daylight, cold.
Base of the door a deep, dark hole revealed,
rising, a wall of ivy, thick and old.

Resting on narrow ledges, Rudi climbed
the ivy-covered wall, so old and high.
Scrambling and pulling fingers, toes were cold,
finally glimpsed the tree tops and the sky.

Climbing down, fearful, his feet touched the earth,
walked through the forest; falling leaves of brown,
of russet red and yellow turned through air,
marking their whirling dance through vale and town.

Rudi walked on through forest, weary way.
Many a twisted path was turned around,
teased by the whistling Auka, sprite of green.
Many the nettled grove he tumbled down.

Blurred was the creature Rudi came upon.
Dashed past his face, with hot breath, touching fear.
Then a small dog with bright red teeth appeared
and Rudi knew the Volkolak was near.

Fast Rudi ran, through prickly leaves and twigs,
heart fit to burst, a thumping bumping sound.
Could not outrun the Volkolak so swift,
knew that by water was his safer ground.

Sparkling with sunshine was the running brook.
Rudi leaned in and gulped the water fresh.
The Asrai water spirits spoke to him.
Feminine voices whispered through a mesh.

If you can face the Volkolak alone,
hold back your fear and make your heart be bold,
Asrai will hold the creature in its light.
Using your courage – magic will enfold.

Fear tapped his shoulder when the creature came.
Volkolak twisted, misty, running by,
growling and fierce and wrapped around his feet,
snarling, a vortex black and red of eye.

Into this whirlpool, Widow Witch appeared,
cloak of black feathers, eyes of birds – aflame,
mouth yawning fire and arms of silver spears,
feared for her power, also for her name.

Blast at the blood throat, shrieking howl and claws,
sword-tipped, the flashing metal of her arm,
Widow Witch danced the screaming of the sky,
screeching, then silence followed; all was calm.

Time sent a frozen village back to field,
calling the flowers of the field by name.
Widow Witch bit the wolf and saved the boy,
showing her power and – by grace – her fame.

Some say he made it back to tell the tale.
Some say the Widow Witch has kept him – hers.
Some say they fell in love and spirits are.
Some say he is – *the Widow Witch's Curse.*

Other poems

The usual diseases

This house is old.
It creaks and sighs at night and yields its secrets, slowly.
Sometimes they arrive by post.
Accumulated papers,
written long ago, that no one wants.

They tell a story of a man and woman.
A history, a glimpse that comes with deeds,
certificated.
He died young, of the usual diseases,
is what the paper could have said.
The heart, sclerotic, the lungs too full of smoky buses,
soot and coal.

Left her to live on, in empty rooms, her widowhood.
To pay the mortgage, she must go each week,
to get the stamp to prove he's dead.
The company would pay, begrudgingly,
they must, and stamp her card.
And they would make her pay.
One quarter of a century and more she lived on,
staring out of the window, smoking the hours away.
What did she think about?

Toothbrush

In the old days
we read books, lit candles,
wrote letters, sent postcards, washed clothes by hand,
wired our own plugs and changed our own fuses,
worked a treadle sewing machine just for the fun of it,
washed our own dishes, mended jumpers, bought mothballs.
Black balaclavas were innocent head warmers that boys wore
    in winter time.
Record players were high tech.
Starlings were noisy and came out in twilight, to deafen the
    buildings in town.
Birds pecked the milk tops and drank from the bottle.
Sparrows were everywhere.
Hard drive was a journey and no one was woken, five a.m., by
    a toothbrush
gone bonkers and will not shut off,
rattling bathroom jar, this is technology, betrayed by
    Prometheus.
Change is a good thing, they say.

Blue tablecloth

When I found you,
inanimate but full of movement
tablecloth of blue flowers, vintage shop in Prague,
I thought ... *Where have you been?*
All this time you have lain, like a secret, amongst the silks and
    fine linens,
safe in your deep drawer, cool and dark,
protected
while villages burned and military puppets marched and died
    into history.

You are brand new, without a brand,
your makers' mark a tiny paper label, glued, of pencilled
    numbers.
You are new but old, without the particles of life ingrained.
You are linen, woven with the printer's ink.
Were you drawn from life – another secret?
Your cornflower-blue petals defying your true name.
You were meant for some summer table long ago.

Nobody ever spilt coffee on you
or gathered together friends and laughter, red wine on
    drunken nights,
cried over their milk, dropped salt tears on you, thumped a fist
    down in anger,
fell asleep on you.
You never felt the splayed fingers of a baby's table grasp.

I will take you home to a wooden kitchen table
and spill cake crumbs on your fine linen strands
and maybe ... a little red wine.

Biro on cardboard

First trip to San Francisco, cafe on a pier.
A beggar is working the tables.
He gets to us ...
Gimme a dollar, he wails.
He's thin and very dirty, long hair,
he looks like Jesus in a white man's kind of way.

My friend resists, the beggar stays,
a stand-off now.
Gimme a dollar,
the beggar, like a robot, does not waiver,
but my friend, he will not give.

The beggar speaks from somewhere,
I'm a Vietnam veteran.
I don't think so, mutters my friend.

Years later in the city, things have improved for beggars
with cardboard placards, pitches
on busy corner pavements
with biro scrawled on cardboard,
I am a cancer survivor.

Outside

Outside the karaoke bar:
full sport coverage, happy hour, giant screen,
pints one pound,
it's raining a grey blanket Saturday.

As the taxi glides to a stop, the boys turn from across the road,
like a missile, radar on.
From the cab, two girls emerge,
arranging their bodies with skeletal grace
of milk-white flesh, mannequin thinness,
exotic gazelles,
barely covered.
The boys crack out a braying howl of a wolf,
that turns, full-throated,
lusty, challenging.
The girls don't blink, but grasp their purses
and stalk towards the neon of the bar.

Tripwire

If words were bullets, there'd be blood on the ground
and family honour's been floating around.
It's been up, down, nailed to the ground.
The feeling of fury doesn't make a sound.

Empty train carriage on a quiet way.
His voice holds fast, though the green fields sway,
past churches and children come out to play.
As calm as tripwire, on this sunny day.

I told you I was gay, when there was time to say.
If I was down in the gutter, you would turn away,
so I really don't care what you have to say.
You can come to my wedding or you can stay away.

Concise field guide

Some are twisted, gnarled, like an old cactus tree
the demons visible, gawping and gasping for air, through grey
   tangled wood.
Some are spiky, with thorns that will get you,
armour-plated, like an ancient rose, out to draw blood.
Some are poisonous as the yew, with its waxy red berries,
   malignant.
Some are unkempt, like the ragged robin, bright as a party babe,
   shredded by life.
Some come creeping, sly like bindweed, in pink and white
   trumpets,
disguising invasion plans.

Some are strong, feeding others, like bugle,
in sweet hidden places by streams or in churchyards.
Some are plenty, like pignut and yarrow, have much grace and
   beauty.
Some are magical, crimson, like great burnet,
a science fiction lollipop from outer space.
Some are camouflaged in plain sight,
the soft green palette of the tortoise beetle on the leaf.
Some are beautiful, like the nodding harebell, from which,
   midsummer nights, we drift
and when the winter moon rises, scattered by clouds, we
   dream of the harebell
or the magic lantern of fritillary, hanging its head like a
   ballerina.
Exotic, as from some distant land,
when all the time, it's been here, hidden.

For each, we were not born to die

When I did that thing,
that thing that women do.
Emerging
between the membrane,
to give the perfect gift.

Suddenly,
an impossible, monstrous thought
came lurching by.
That for each soldier who fell,
the battlefield.
That for each man
a woman laboured long,
and hope and fear and raging pain
all took their turn,
to give this world a miracle.
To give the perfect gift.

And for the first time
I knew the pity and the anger.

Tales from the nail bar

Hot sun through plate glass windows.

The nail bar doors are open to the street.

The staff are studiously filing, painting, fixing nail tips.

Tattooed man walks in: he's young, big shoulders and long
    legs,

tagged, on his ankle.

Tall in shorts and vest – built for playing basketball,

front teeth missing and cheerfully asking,

Ain't ya done yet ... shall I go back to t' boozer?

Laughing, four-letter words into his mobile,

loud about the *200 bar* he's owed.

Customers are scowling quietly.

His girlfriend, left cheek big crucifix tattoo, and swallows,
    necked,

her face, cut like a glacier

and getting nails to match.

Old lady struggles in, her tartan shopping bag on wheels.

She asks, *What da moat you pay fah paytin nays?*

she has no teeth. The Thai staff have no words.

I translate ... the cost is seven pounds.

She turns and leaves.

I notice that her blouse, caramel in colour, of lace and beaded
    chiffon,

is beautiful as it moves in the breeze.

The petit bourgeois way of doing things

How far apart they are, how ripped apart they are.
Remote as stars at night.
Supermarket hum of women's voices,
two friends chatting,
just past the deli counter.

The boy in the hoody pulled his jacket up so tight.
Package wrinkled, plastic crinkled,
how I noticed, yes, that's right.
Shoved the pork pies up his jacket
hands in pockets, turned,
took flight.

She was wearing this season's colours in the cafe.
Talking vintages and how she loved those Saturdays,
drinking the best champagne …
and something irritable in her voice.

How far apart they are.
The champagne lady and the shoplifter.
How far apart they are, how ripped apart they are.
Remote as stars at night.

Rosa

Rosa Parks was a woman, she was very strong,
she had courage ten miles long.
She had courage ten miles long.
Now what kind of world were they living for –
a world corrupted, a world so poor?
By cruel turns of history,
poor reality, poor reality.

The driver he said, *Go to the door, use the other door, use the
other door.*
Worked all day, she couldn't stand no more.
Worked all day, she couldn't take no more.
She said *No!*
She said *No!*

Rosa Parks was a woman, she was very strong,
she had courage ten miles long.

Dreams

When the gods first made us, we were supernovae.
Atoms held together.
We were born from the stars.
We shot out when the stars exploded.
Diamonds in the snow.

We grew from black volcanoes.
We were the noble dreams.
Then came the fall
and our hearts turned hard like crystal.

But in the house of dreams,
you climbed the mountains at the dusty feet of the gods.

You looked down over the valley
and saw the sky and saw the stars,
glittering.

The many love letters of Rosa Luxembourg

When you are not here
I lie very still in the darkness
and imagine that I can hear you breathing.
In time, I can hear you breathing.
It becomes
this moment.
Like being in a room and hearing the ocean outside.
Hearing the dull hoosh hoosh, through the night.
Knowing that it's real,
though you cannot see it.

I imagine the shape of you.
The small rise and fall in the quiet of blankets.
I look for the shape of your coat on the hook by the door.

I ask myself, *What can history tell us,*
as we struggle for freedom for everyone?
Not knowing how long we have
and what we might have, in a different life.

When you are here,
you will lean over in the darkness
and touch my lips
for one moment.

.

Wheelchair blues

You become invisible
when you're in a wheelchair.
People too busy, through walkways and doorways,
exits and entrances,
don't look.
They just see a man pushing somebody,
Blink out, blank out.

So, there in the food hall, by the flowers, waiting
near to the checkout, with nothing to do.
A young girl is staring,
maybe she's noticed
my foot in its plaster cast
and I hope I look friendly
in my funny hat, wool hat,
ears like Koala bear.
I smile,
she frowns ... looks away.

Canal

Canal towpath
looks like the party died last year.
Water is the only thing that seems alive.
There is lanceolate yellow of struggling hawks' beard
in the mutant half-light.
Green is green,
valiant, despite the meagre grey,
before the March winds begin to ruffle the grass
and give blue light to sky.

Blood on grass and violence.
Casual.
Dead sheep, white and waxy
in a corner field.
Past the carcass of a mallard.
Fox got it, he says.

I imagine a large white rabbit,
perhaps.
A particularly vicious cartoon rabbit
with werewolf teeth,
lolloping over the field.
Red stains on grass, blood and feathers.
Blink, don't want to think.

Night ward

Suddenly they are gone and I'm alone.
Night ward at 3 a.m.
Dark, but lights are bleeping red, electric bulbous, in the
    ceiling.
In the shadows across the room, some light is flickering.
Pain-scratched brain makes a leap into the unknown,
thinks, light is the glow from a mobile phone.
As if that bundle of covers across the room
could be checking her texts under the sheets.

Those who look after us are some distance away,
around a bending corridor.
But through the dark, loud voices carry
a fountain of juggling words.
The tone is light, dedicated, continuous,
betraying any chance of silence.
The buzzer for the toilet rings and rings
before some feet and clanging noise.

My sleepless brain delves into memory of other wards I've
    known,
brings up a filmic shot of rows of sleeping bodies in their beds.
The ranks arranged in order from the door – most serious to
    least.
Ward Sister swoops with eagle eyes, to check
one night nurse, chair, alone.
A desk, a metal table lamp the only light.

Across the room the bundle of covers is praying audibly,
sometimes mumbling.

I'm sorry to be asking you again, but please can you help me
through this ...

and if you can help me through this ...

The words come round and round again.

Next door is crying.

The morphine is not working.

The nurses tell her it's anxiety, but they will give her
something.

Next door is crying.

I am praying for the codeine to kick in.

After the catastrophe

After the catastrophe, foot held a meeting.
The usual muscles were there, flexor, fibularis and tibialis.
Everyone had frozen and no one could move well at all.
The muscles grumbled: an interloper was living upstairs!
As if that wasn't bad enough, there was more than one of them.
They're all weird, tall things with many little ones attached!
Came from somewhere after the big sleep.
We blame them for all the pain! cried the flexors.
That's not true, said Achilles, who was sulking at the back.
It's me you have, to tend on you,
if you play the blame game.
If you want paralysing power and thunder
then I'm the one and I'm your number.
But we haven't got room for them, the muscles cried.
It's overcrowding, we can't cope!
And what the hell is titanium anyway?
Enough of this, said foot.
We need each other
or we'll fall apart.
We have to learn again to move as one.
We have to learn to live together, we need each other.
Slowly, they began to get along.

The iceberg

Going to visit the aged mountain
when the days were like a measuring tape.
Knowing that the crack will appear
and you will suffer again like a child on tiptoe.

Behind the bouquets, the betrayal,
lie complicated dreams.
Give me your bleeding heart, mouthing regret.
An embarrassing uncontrolled muscle.

Two-spot ladybird

I thank you
two-spot ladybird
for being here.
You are sexy, like a new, red cup.
Deep scarlet and those crazy spots.
And what about those legs,
industriously searching the window pane.
I found one of you resting on my duvet in February.
Usually, you are carpet sleeping by the skirting board.
You are always out partying when you shouldn't be,
hanging out, sunbathing in inappropriate places
out of season.
If you were human
you would be out
dancing in November,
wearing only a little black lace.

Ladybird, don't leave.

Boxing match

On the outside, she looks calm.
But inside her head, it's like a boxing match.
Angry little monkey ball of screwed-up fury.
Gloves on, knuckles clenched,
and in the red corner ... *Ladies and gentlemen*.

And now the bouncing
into the white, mad mist.
But not like that Scorsese movie,
where Robert De Niro danced
with balletic grace, like some medieval monk,
as molecules of dust floated in light and time and space.
No,
more like an angry little monkey ball of screwed-up fury.

America

In the baking heat
We auto past the humble cabins of the American Dream.
Forests go by and hours of towering pine trees go by.
The cabins dash past, flying the flag.
Hamlets of timber shacks and fences,
but always a church or two, freshly painted.
Grey cables loop the highway,
like curtains, these arteries, thick and brown.
Industrial, strangely crude, against the green abundant trees.

Then we get to Dollywood,
which lingers on for miles.
The shocking, neon pink.
The foothills of the Great Smoky Mountains,
blue and misty grey.

October

Wild, angry clouds are pushing the sky around.
Amber, russet, red, the leaves fly by the window,
sharp against the green grass.
The last gift of autumn here, in the graceful pink of roses,
slightly scabby from the wind.

The black cat cries outside on the window sill,
pleading for entry into the warmth.
Her cat breath moment is small
heat on the window pane.
She makes mouth-shaped kisses
appear and then vanish
from the glass.

The radio was singing

Were you dreaming of the desert in the thin October sunshine
when you married me,
when you married me?

Were you thinking of tomorrow, were you planning for your
    lost life?
Like a poet in the desert, finding freedom in the mountains
and the sky,
romance in the struggle?

Bowie sang so sweetly on the morning of my wedding.
The radio was singing, *Get me to the church on time.*
My belly was the measure of a full half-moon of baby.

The day was full of flowers and happiness and laughter.
But you built a wall around you, with your Berlin heart
still bleeding on your sleeve and dreaming,
like a refugee.

Never stop

It was a good year for the criminals,
the dirty money, sloshing around, washed and pressed.
It was a good year for the corporate.
Those golden eggs.

It was a good year for the waistcoats.
Sitting on committees with nothing left to say,
but to keep the state of play
for a thousand pounds a day.

Not a bad year for the Eton boys,
smiling like schoolboys,
buttoned up and smirking
from the corners of their mouths.

Was a bad year for the homeless.
Those days of cuts and cuts,
and a worse year for the refugees,
who wore the colour scapegoat.

In the Bible, people washed away their sins
on a creature sent out to the desert.
So when they lay all the sins of the world upon you,
what colour is the colour scapegoat?

Mirror pool

First time out in sandals without inviting frostbite,
this Yorkshire April sunshine belies an arctic wind.
The toddlers whoop and chatter while troughing through
    the water,
the mirror pool is sparkling, children soaked to the skin.

An old man stops to chat now, says, *It's bikini weather,*
how he misses his wife now, how he'd love to have her back.
I see the careful clothing, the whiteness of his collar,
the kindly face, the laughter and the walking stick.

He gestures with his stick now towards the pub to go to –
ah, but which pub to go to? Now that's the crux of it.
Says, *When they named that pub there*
they must have been … must have been …
Aye, must have been twelve sheets to the wind.

Sunday morning

The tribes gathered, walking beyond the grieving stones.
Some came in sombre dress, others in rainbow clothes.
Slowly, we climbed the slippery wet grass,
in light rain, to an unknown place.
We searched each other's faces, held hands.

Up to a clearing, circled
by slender branches of young woodland.
A light breeze blew up, then faded away.
I imagined you there, singing and dancing,
dressed in your best gown of glittering stars.
Gold and silver falling from your feet.

Scudding past Saturday, the sky, cold and wind-blown, blue.
Seaside cliffs, screeching gulls, crashing waves
rising up, pulling apart, over the ocean floor.
Sea-green aventurine
beating out the rhythms in the shrill air.

York by train

The woman on the train, she was talking to the dog.
She was talking to the dog.
She was talking to the dog.
She was talking.
And he said and she said and he said and she said.
The woman on the train, she was talking to the dog,
just as if ... he was a real person.

The woman on the train, she was crying out loud,
she was cursing out loud on her mobile phone,
as the green fields rushed past the window glass
and the sodden grass was wet with rain.
Didn't cry on trains, didn't cry on trains,
they hid their pain like running away.
Might have died on trains
but didn't cry on trains,
didn't cry on trains, didn't cry on trains
didn't cry on trains
didn't cry on trains.

York by day, York by day.
By gothic Minster stone, by mullioned window rose,
the drunken revellers posed,
hen party ... liquored up
stiletto, killer walk
on pincers as they stalk
with plastic sex toy – pink –
he was upside down in drink,
with legs akimbo, think they were talking to the doll.

They were talking to the doll
they were talking to the doll
they were talking to the doll
just as if ... he was a real person.

Our Tracey's Google

On the coach from the shiny airport, it's seventy degrees
    of jet lag.
We are sun-starved, weary northerners,
with refugees from the Hebrides, wrapped up in fur lined
    thermals ...
and still thawing out.

Charming and disarming, in vintage polyester –
two trouser-suited ladies of a certain age.
Powder blue, the pastel and ghosting for Alan Bennett,
discussing hip replacements, remembering past conquests
and every trim young waiter they have flirted with.

They've done it and they've seen it and they even bought
    the T-shirt
and now they're talking laptops, like two old office techies,
intoning words and phrases, impressive is their courage
in embracing all the changes in the mellow years,
    the mellow years.

And then they get to Google, and then they get to Google.
Well ... *If you cannot find it, you can always look on Tracey's,*
on our Tracey's Google, on our Tracey's Google.
And a myriad of Googles unfolds before the senses
and how I wish I had one to nurse me through the changes,
as I learn to walk on stilts now, whilst balancing an orange
    on my head.

I love these Yorkshire ladies, they're like New Age
    Ena Sharples,

they've jettisoned the hairnet for the power curl and laptop

and they're not afraid to say so and they're loud and gauche
    and funny

and they'll keep on Greece-and-Spaining it, for as long as
    there's the money.

The recusants

For we must keep the Queen from those who plan to harm
and we must keep the King from Popish Plots and we must
make a law that governs all and makes it clear that you must
go to church or face the harm of proof and penalty of law;
a subject, who does not love Church and King.

After the old abbey went, folk held on to their ways.
In the rough northern hills, where the wind burned your face
and the darkness closed in, here was trouble and more for
    authority.
In the wild woods live unconformity.
Those who sold potions of yarrow, herb robert, cowslip,
dead nettle, were named cunning men and named cunning
    women
and knew how to heal, with hands and with nature.

Some offered spells and charms, walking a fine line
between exchange of goods or food, or ending in the pillory
or foul Lancaster gaol, accused of sorcery.
Or off to York Assizes they would go,
in wretched poverty,
a treason, to think differently.

Old women, bent like a longbow and furrowed with years,
healers and menders, and midwives and running the risk
of malice from others, in the seeds of the heart.
The ailing cow, the sudden death, the illness without name.
Loss, chasing blame, the practisers of magic arts,
charmers and enchanters, the toad, the cat, the pins in clay.

The tapestry of wicked lies, elaborate, with jealousy.
The feuding clans suggested words from mouth to ear
leaked evil.
Vile imp, dressed as sanctimony, drew the blade, the knife,
the cut
and names spilled out.

*In Malkin Tower they met one night, the witches' coven
in plain sight ...*
And fanciful, the stories grew, of feasting and of Satan.
But all accused and this, the naming – by one child of nine.
Condemned they were, by Jennet.

Who tutored Jennet, while her mother lay in prison cell?
Squintin' Lil, as she was known,
whose eye lopsided downward in her face.
Malicious laughs and sneering faces,
and Jennet, the bastard child.

Who tutored Jennet so she pointed out, so clear of voice,
her mother, brother, sister – all her family –
as witches, quite disgusting and most foul their deadly deeds?
Condemned them all she did, in court with pointing finger,
an orphan, by her words.

And after all the hanging done, who took her in,
the pointing finger?
How did she live, this child of Malkin Tower?
A hovel, clinging to a hill.

And what did Jennet think, two decades on,
before she too, was bound for prison cell?
Accused upon the word of yet another child.

For we must keep the Queen from those who plan to harm
and we must keep the King from Popish Plots and we must
make a law that governs all and makes it clear that you must
go to church or face the harm of proof and penalty of law;
a subject, who does not love Church and King.

Jennet's evidence in the 1612 Pendle witch trial in Lancashire led to the execution of ten people, including all of her own family. Recusant was the name given to people who did not attend the Church of England, when it was compulsory to do so.

Magazine dreams

Long before the world changed
and we began to worry for the oceans and the trees,
it was fern for the bathroom and bamboo for the lounge,
and a scrubbed pine kitchen was there for the longing.
Imagining those perfect spaces
to lay claim to dreams.

But the solid oak kitchen won't save you now
from the shadows in the bathroom.
And even extensive white marble won't deliver you
from the grey ghost in the corner
of desirable colours and the cushions of affluence.

In the scrubbed-pine theory of life,
you can have everything that you might have wanted.
Every bauble of success.
You can lose and you can choose to screw it all and
throw your life to the wind.
So you can breathe again.

Ludwig, part one

Because of all the words you never said,
we are condemned to scratch the itch,
and we will scratch until it bleeds.
We know no other way.

Mystery

Because the monsters shot your father dead.
The shock lay like a broken bird in snow.
It took us forty years to learn the truth.
Understanding little.

Memory

The ghost of those imagined, different deaths
that haunted you throughout your adult life.
The noble ways to die are always best.
Heroic and fulfil the lie.

Dignity

The ones who made you watch – and you a boy.
A yard, a firing squad, some soldiers, this is what she said,
but never of the prison cell and time you spent.
They threw away the key.

The mother tongue you kept close to your breast.
The silent, barbed-wire thoughts were always close.
The stories have a life that twists and turns.
Memories rewind.

Ludwig, part two

Son, she wrote,
this is how they murdered your father
and five years of praying have brought me nothing
    but grey hair
and God is jealous in his love.

Through the darkness the soldiers trudged, with shovels
    and machine guns.
Captive to the night and the broken buildings.
Surrounded.
It was cold and the trees were black with stars.
Death was waiting in the yawning, grin, jaw,
    guerra.

To freeze the heart, starlight, say goodbye.
The trees were all they saw.

A different story.
They drove and the shovels clap-clapping hard upon the boards
in the truck, into the forest.
Or like that drawing by Goya, scratched, a man, blindfolded,
    slumps,
tied to this earth and not tied.
Or that last cigarette, the narrative of execution.
Or maybe a different canvas:
a high wall, some trees, sunshine,
a warm summer morning.

Antique rose

I loved her dear
but not my idea, to parcel out her ashes to all the sisters.
I planted mine beneath a rose bush, ruby in its velvet lush.
Antique red rose bush, with armour-plated thorns,
would take a swipe at me, like some vengeful, ancient ancestor,
each time I got too near.

Tall and sturdy
slender and unbreakable, this rose,
like the roses she once grew, I am reminded.
Victoria or Edward, they bloomed in myriad hues
of pinks and reds in perfect borders,
untouchable.

Polish Anna

She was called Polish Anna, came to England then Bradford.
Post-war life, in hostels, a human reminder
of horrors untold.

Was once a young woman, with youth and a big smile,
always in the market, for she made it her day home.
She was huge, kind of scary and built like a mountain,
but she smiled and she laughed, shook her stick wildly
    and shouted at people
and she often talked to herself.

Alarming some shoppers, beguiling stall holders,
amongst all the people, between chickens and pork pies,
    apples and oranges,
she was there and market traders' kindness looked after her.
She wore lots of badges, lapels on her jackets
to show she was happy and belonged.

Looked like she was homeless, with her mind full of puzzles,
alarming some shoppers, beguiling stall holders
into giving her hot cups of tea.

She was tough, European, like the people she'd come from
and always the knowing what the years and the horrors
    had done .
She smiled and she laughed and she banged her stick loudly.
She was one crazy lady and most people feared her
and most people loved her, for they knew, without knowing
what the years and the horrors had done.

Voices

Where is my home among the forests?
I have forgotten where the mountains are.
My father coughs and curses British weather.
I wonder what my village looks like now.

The soldiers came and all the sky grew purple
and clouds of rain came down upon my face.
What is it that holds us all together
under the skin, the blood, the bone, the race?

Where am I now and is this my beginning?
I live here now and learn to love the place.
The seasons change, but must not choose forgetting,
yet go about the world and find your place.

.

Between

Between the iceberg and the volcano
there must be a calmer path,
where you are not in danger of the burning,
or becoming so little that the Ice Queen will forget you.
She probably considered it all one morning, on her way
    to work.
Then decided it was not worth it.
Who wants to live with ice monsters anyway?